Sylvie PERSEC

CORRIGÉS DES EXERCICES

Grammaire raisonnée 1

anglais

Lycée - Niveau B1 à B2
du Cadre européen commun
de référence pour les langues

Nouvelle
édition
augmentée

OPHRYS

© **Éditions Ophrys**
ISBN : 978-2-7080-0951-6

Ophrys - 5, avenue de la République - 75011 Paris

CHAPITRE I

P. 7 Exercice niveau I
2. a) Does he like her?
   b) Is he talking to her?
   c) Has he seen them?
   d) Are they working with Alice.
   e) Have they sent a new message?
   Exercice niveau 2
4. Dear Emma,
   Have you really made up your mind how you feel? **Do** you know how I feel?
   The same way as I **did** the night we first met. I **didn't** think I'd write to you
   again, but now I **have** done it.
   Do you want to see me next week or **don't** you? If I **don't** hear from you in
   a few days, I'll know. **Don't** worry, you'll never hear from me again.
   John

P. II Exercice niveau I
2. **Valeur des formes en contexte**

	a) une action habituelle	b) une caractéristique (quasi-) permanente du sujet	c) un événement unique à l'intérieur d'un récit
I enter ...			X
... buy ...			X
... works ...		X	
... go ...			X
... like ...		X	
... use ...	X		
... get out ...			X
... get ...			X
... descend ...			X
... fills in ...			X

Exercice niveau 2
4. - When I **feel** lonely, I **try** to remember that I still **have** my daughter with me.
   - **Doesn't** she want a career?
   - Not really. At the moment she**'s working** on her research and that makes
     her quite happy.
   - What **is** she **working** on?
   - Something to do with Paris.
   - I suppose she **has** to go abroad for her research sometimes.
   - Well, no, she **manages** to do most of the work here.

P. 13 Exercice niveau 2

2. Jonathan is a representative of PLAN International which is a charity working with children and their families in poor countries.
"Jonathan, what is PLAN International about?"
"Well, we **know** that we cannot really help the world's poor by simply giving them money. And we **do not want** to impose Western solutions on them. Of course, we often **give** medicines and some of the basic things people need But in most cases, we **try** to teach people the skills they **need**."
"Can you give me an example?"
"Well, at the moment in Africa, we**'re giving** people the chance to improve their own lives. Right now, we**'re helping** 200 village people in Tanzania to build their own school. To give just another example:
in the Embu area of Kenya we**'re helping** to equip a clinic and to build tanks to conserve rainwater."
"**Do** you always **teach** people the same skills?"
"Of course not. It always **depends** on what the local people want to do."
"**Do** you **want** people to make their own choices?"
"Yes. When we **arrive** in a village, we always **talk** to the village leaders. And they **tell** us what they need."
"**Do** you **think** that PLAN International can really make things better?"
"Yes, definitely."
"What are your plans for the future?"
"Well, at the moment I**'m trying** to develop child sponsorship.
I**'m seeing** some of the Kenyan government's representatives next week. I'm very hopeful."

P. 15 Exercice niveau 1

2. 1. b) do you think
   2. b) are you thinking
   3. b) Are ... seeing
   4. b) 's having
   5. a) have
   Exercice niveau 2

4. The blue whale **migrates** each year from the polar regions to the sub-tropics. It **starts** from Iceland and **reaches** warmer waters later in the year. Scientists have just been told that a new species of whale **is** now **travelling** in the waters of the Antartic. It **seems** that the new species is a cross between whales and dolphins. Scientists **are studying** the problem very seriously.

P. 17 Exercice niveau 1

2. 1. What time **did** the boy **go** into the building?
   2. Who(m) **did** Jordan **see**?
   3. **Did** Jordan walk **away**?
   4. What **did** Jordan **hear**?
   5. **Did** Jordan **use** his gun?

5. **Exercice niveau 2**

An angry mum **demanded** an inquiry after her three-year-old daughter **was left** behind on a school outing. Little Ann Marie was in tears as she **watched** the coach that **was carrying** her 27 schoolmates leave without her. When the staff at the zoo **found** Ann Marie one hour after the departure of the coach, the little girl **was sitting** on the ground and still **crying**. They **tried** to comfort her by giving her some sweets. But it **took** them quite a long time to calm her down. Teachers only **found** she was missing two hours later when they **arrived** at the village school 60 miles away.

P. 19 **Exercice niveau I**

2. Two British tourists **were killed** in Majorca on New Year's Eve. The murderers **entered** the tourists' villa in the small hours of the morning. They **stole** the couple's belongings and then **stabbed** to death Edith and John Loader. A few hours after the murder **took** place Inspector Juan Feliz **declared**: "We very much regret the events of last night. We **have** already **arrested** a few suspects. We **haven't identified** the murderers yet. But the criminals will be punished."

Exercice niveau 2

4. It is 80 years to the day since a primary school teacher called Valentine Robinson **founded** the charity Save the Children. She **was born** on 27 August 1870 and **died** in 1950. She **went** to Cambridge University and then **became** a school teacher. She never **married** instead she **devoted** her life to helping children. During World War One she **launched** the first official fund appeal. Since then the charity **has tried** to help other needy children in England and abroad. In 1921 Valentine Robinson **wrote** down guidelines for treating the world's children. These **have been** the basis for a number of international conventions on children's rights which **have** already **been signed** by a large number of countries.

P. 21 **Exercices niveau I**

2. 1. Where **did they spend** their holidays last year?
   2. You're late! **We've** already **had** lunch.
   3. What **happened** to him after he left her?
   4. **I've just spoken** to him! He says it's OK.
3. "Nowadays lots of people **say** that the Internet **has changed** the way we **work**. It **seems** to me that it **has changed** more than that. It **has** already **created** a new lifestyle and a new way of communicating."

Exercice niveau 2

5. 1. "When we **married**, Diane never **entertained** the thought that our children would ever want to live anywhere else - her family **have (has) been** here since the 1870s - but now she **has begun** searching for available properties in other cities."
   2. "I **have** now **lived** (**have been living**: possible mais moins probable ici) in the area for some 31 years. The last time I **resolved** to leave town was in 1968 when, as a 19-year-old college student, I **worked** for the local newspaper. I **was** at the Ambassador Hotel on June 5 when the editor **had** a heart attack."

P. 23 Exercices niveau I

3. 1. They **have been** there for two hours. Ils sont là depuis deux heures.
   2. I **have been living** here for four weeks. J'habite ici depuis quatre semaines.
   3. I **haven't seen** her since Monday. Je ne l'ai pas vue depuis lundi.
   4. I**'ve been waiting** two hours. J'attends depuis deux heures.
   5. They**'ve been working** with us for two weeks. Ils travaillent avec nous depuis deux semaines.

4. 1. Who are they? They've been here for a week.
   2. Where is she? I haven't seen her since last week.
   3. They've lived (they've been living) with us for two months.
   4. He's been watching her for ten minutes.

Exercice niveau 2

6. 1. He doesn't want to see us. We haven't seen him for two months.
   2. He's very late. I've been waiting for him for two hours.
   3. I wonder what they've been doing all afternoon!
   4. You've been drinking! Look at yourself in the mirror!
   5. He's eaten three cakes (forme be+ing impossible ici à cause de l'expression d'une quantité précise).
   6. I've watched (I've been watching) your film. I liked it very much (le prétérit renvoie au moment - passé - où l'on a regardé le film).

P. 25 Exercice niveau I

3. On June 3, Jonathan Robinson **was arrested** because he **had caused** an accident on the London Road two months before. Yesterday he **was sentenced** to six months in jail after telling the magistrates that he **had had** four or five glasses of wine just before leaving his home on the night of the accident. He also said that he **had eaten** nothing at all that day.

Exercice niveau 2

5. When the earth shook...
   "My family **happened** to be out of town on the morning of the earthquake; I **had taken** Diane, my wife and three children along with me for a lecture in Florida. When we **returned** home two days after the quake we **found** our house blessedly unscarred: a few wine bottles and some glassware **had fallen** from shelves but the damage **remained** minimal. Nevertheless, several rooms looked as if they **had been ransacked**."
   From The Sunday Times, 23 January 1994

CHAPITRE 2

P. 29 Exercice niveau 1
  2. 1. I saw him two days ago.
      2. How long ago did you talk to him? (How long has it been since you last talked to him?)
      3. He phoned me two days ago. I never saw him again afterwards.
      4. He came after dinner. Then we watched a film.
      5. When I met him two months ago, he was twenty years old.
  Exercice niveau 2
  4. 1. They sold the house two months ago. Then they left for Spain.
      2. What did you do after talking (after you talked) to her?
      3. - "How long ago did he write to you ?"
         - "A long time ago."
      4. After her daughter was born, she bought a new car.
      5. It happened after Clare's departure.
      6. After writing to him/her, she went out.
      7. He came back after talking to him/her (after he had talked to him/her).

P. 31 Exercice niveau 1
  2. 1. He always goes out in the evening.
      2. She left two years ago, but her brother is still here
      3. I haven't seen him yet.
      4. You've seen him before in some place.
      5. Sorry! I've already finished.
  Exercices niveau 2
  4. 1. You can stay **as long as** you wish; a month, a year if you like.
      2. **As soon as** I arrived home, I went to bed.
      3. **As** he had had too much to drink, his friend drove him home.
      4. **As** he wished to leave early, he packed his case the day before.
  5. 1. It will not happen as long as I **live**.
      2. He decided that he would do it as soon as he **arrived**.
      3. As the years **passed**, she grew more and more desperate.
      4. He realized that he **had met** her before.
      6. She won't leave before she **has seen** him.

P. 33 Exercice niveau 1
  2. 1. Have you **ever** been to Australia?
      2. I have **never** talked to him.
      3. She's met him **before**.
      4. It's the most important thing I have **ever** seen.
      5. I'll do it **before** you leave.
  Exercice niveau 2
  4. 1. He talked to us for ten minutes during the conference.
      2. Have you ever read a story like that?
      3. I'll leave before the end of the film. Don't go to sleep before (until) I come back.
      4. I've never talked to her. I don't think I've ever met anybody like her.
      5. It's the worst thing you've ever done.

P. 35 Exercice niveau 1

4. Alison David started singing a long time **ago**. She's been singing jazz **since** 1995. She had her first album out five years **ago**. **Since** then, she has recorded two other albums. She's been touring Europe **for** five years now.

Exercice niveau 2

6. Paul Hutchinson **started** his campaign against the slaughter of dolphins many years ago. For five days in October 1991 he **filmed** hundreds of dolphins trapped in fishermen's nets in the Pacific. Since his film **was released**, thousands of people **have joined** in the campaign for the protection of dolphins.

P. 37 Exercice niveau 1

2. "Over the past two or three years, many people **have accused** the Internet of ruining the art of conversation. But I **don't agree** with them. So far, the Internet **has helped** millions of people to communicate. As a result, the net **has developed** new skills and new attitudes. I **have had** a computer since 1992 and I **have had** an E-mail address since last year."

4. Exercice niveau 2
   1. He's been at home for two weeks (now).
   2. How long has he been ill (now)?
   3. How often does he come here?
   4. She has changed a lot over the past few months.
   5. How long have they been on holiday (now)?

P. 39 Exercice niveau 2

3. 1. Once he **has passed** his exams, he'll be qualified for the job.
   2. I know that as soon as he **gets** there he will feel better.
   3. As long as you **stay** with them, you'll be all right.
   4. He said he would stay till I **arrived**.
   5. They told me I was to go once I **had finished**.
   6. Don't leave until you **have finished**.
   7. - "When will you do it?"
      - "As soon as you **stop** asking me!"

P. 41 Exercice niveau 1

2. 1. I haven't seen her yet!
   2. You're smoking again!
   3. He's still asleep.
   4. I've been here for two days (now).
   5. She waited (she's waited) for me for two hours.
   6. He has always liked cats.

Exercices niveau 2

4. Paul Ross started his anti-smoking campaign ten years ago. Two years later, he began to talk on CNN. He has already written two books. Every week, for thirty minutes, young people ask him questions on the radio. "I've smoked for two years. My parents smoked for twenty years. What can I do to quit?"

5. 1. She has been living here since last summer.
   2. It's been raining since this morning
   3. He's been out (away) for two hours.
   4. He died five years ago.
   5. He's been missing since Saturday.

P. 43 Exercice niveau I

2. 1. État. a) We've been friends for a long time.
2. Fait passé. b) He disappeared three months ago ...
3. État. a) He's been back for two days!
4. Fait passé. b) He came back an hour ago ...

CHAPITRE 3

P. 45 Exercice niveau I

2. 1. - **Do** you often **go** skiing?
- Yes, **I** sometimes **do**. **I** often **go** to Austria and they **have** wonderful skiing resorts there.
2. - **Do** you sometimes **do** the shopping with her?
- No, **I** never **do**.
3. - **Does** he sometimes **have** a drink after work?
- Well, **he** sometimes **goes out** with colleagues.

Exercice niveau 2

4. 1. - You don't like her a lot, do you?
- I **do** like her but she hardly ever speaks to me.
2. - It will never work.
- **Do** try again!
3. - She never answered your letters, did she?
- She **did** answer once. Once only.
4. - He said that he would never leave her.
- Well, he **did** leave her.

P.47 Exercice niveau I

2. 1. **He never talks** to his brother.
2. **Nobody seems** to remember what happened.
3. **I don't know** anybody in this area.
4. **Nothing ever happens** in this town.
5. **He doesn't feel** like joining us.

Exercices niveau 2

5. 1. I'm afraid we don't know them as well as you **do**.
J'ai bien peur que nous ne les connaissions pas aussi bien que vous.
2. "You don't need any help." "No, I **don't**."
« Tu n'as pas besoin d'aide. » « Non. »
3. "Have you ever seen a camel, Susan?" "No, I don't think I **have**."
« As-tu déjà vu un chameau Susan ? » « Non, je ne crois pas. »
4. You don't smoke as much as she **does**.
Tu ne fumes pas autant qu'elle.
5. You say it is too late but I don't think it **is**.
Tu dis que c'est trop tard, mais je ne crois pas.

6. 1. Never had he answered my letters.
2. Only after the press had revealed the case did the President's aides realize they had gone too far.
3. Seldom had I criticized him.
4. No sooner had he arrived than he opened all the windows.

P. 49 Exercice niveau 1

2. *Who did they appoint as head pupil? Who was she chosen by?*
   Who declared that Rosemary was appointed head of school because
   of her integrity and sense of leadership? Why was she was appointed head
   of school?

Exercices niveau 2

4. *1. How long did he stay with them?*
   2. Whose computer is this (is it)?
   3. How is she today?
   4. How far is it from here?
   5. How long ago did he first meet her?

5. *1. Do you know who will be interested in your project?*
   2. Are you ready to face frequent problems?
   3. Do you have financial resources?
   4. Have you got a partner?
   5. Have you ever tried starting a business before?
   6. Do you need financial back up?

P. 51 Exercice niveau 1

1. *1. Q : What colour is it?*
   2. Q : Is it (Was it) expensive?
   3. Q : How much did you pay for it?
   4. Q : How big is it ?
   5. Q : How often do you intend to use it?

Exercice niveau 2

3. *1. Q : How often do you weigh yourself?*
   2. Q : How long can you run without feeling tired?
   3. Q : What's your favourite pastime ?
   4. Q : Why don't you do more exercise?
   5. Q : Where do you usually spend your spare-time?
   6. Q : How many pairs of training shoes do you have?

P. 53 Exercice niveau 1

2. *1. I like football.*
      b) Do you?
      - J'aime le foot.
      - Ah bon ?
   2. - It was a very good film.
      c) No, it wasn't.
      - C'était un très bon film.
      - Non, pas du tout.
   3. - He's very tired.
      a) Yes, he is.
      - Il est très fatigué.
      - Oui.

4. 1. - *You love her, I guess.*
   - Yes, I do.
2. - *Apparently, you don't agree with me.*
   - No, I don't.
3. - *He ended up working with them.*
   - Did he?
4. - *You have agreed to do it!*
   - No, I haven't!

P. 55 Exercice niveau 1
2. 1. - *Will you be at the wedding?*
     a) *I think* **so.**
     - Tu seras au mariage ?
     - Oui, je pense.
   2. - *He loves me.*
     c) *So* **do I.**
     - Il m'aime.
     - Moi aussi.
   3. - *I don't approve of this.*
     b) **Neither** *do I.*
     - Je n'approuve pas cela.
     - Moi non plus.
   4. - *She looked very pretty.*
     c) *So* **did you.**
     - Elle était très jolie.
     - Toi aussi.

Exercice niveau 2
4. 1. - *Don't tell me you did all that work in so little time!*
     - I did, though!
   2. - *You never talked to her, I believe.*
     - Yes, I did!
   3. - *Did she phone him?*
     - I think she did.
   4. - *They probably tried to get in touch with you.*
     - I don't think they did.

P. 57 Exercice niveau 1
2. 1. *Stop laughing,* **will you**?
   2. *He doesn't smoke,* **does he**?
   3. *You like me,* **don't you**?
   4. *You had finished when he came,* **hadn't you**?
   5. *The police came,* **didn't they**?
   6. *You've had a bath,* **haven't you**?
   7. *Start reading,* **will you**?
   8. *We don't have to do it now,* **do we**?
   9. *Let's go,* **shall we**?

3. *"Let's get up on deck, **shall** we?" says his father.*
"We'll find out what's happening." He takes his son's hand.
*"We've had a collision, **haven't** we?," says Mark.*
*"Yes, I think we **have**. But, it's all right."*
*"Hold on to my jacket, **will** you?" says his father. "We ran down a yacht in the fog. We've stopped to pick up the passengers."*
*"They'll never find them in the fog, **will** they?" says Mark.*
*"Of course, they **will**! Look! Here they are!"*
*" They don't know what's happened, **do** they?"*
*"They must be terrified. They nearly died, **didn't** they?"*
*"They're lucky, **aren't** they?"*
*"Yes, I think they **are**."*

P. 59 Exercice niveau 1

2. 1. *Find activities you enjoy!*
   2. *Try dancing or kung-fu!*
   3. *Don't say you don't have time.*
   4. *Don't wait too long!*
   Exercice niveau 2

4. ***Don't panic*** *if you feel an earth tremor! If you're indoors, **stand** in a strong doorway or **get** underneath a table. **Don't go** outside! It could be very risky! **Don't get** in an elevator! That would be the most dangerous thing to do!*
*If you're outdoors and you feel a tremor, **move away** from buildings, trees, brick walls or power lines. If you're driving, **stay in** your car until the shaking has ceased.*

CHAPITRE 4

P. 61 Exercice niveau 2

2.

	Fait passé	Fait irréel
1. ... if your best friend spoke ...		X
2. ... you were more attractive ...		X
3. ... did you last hear ...	X	
4. Suppose you failed ...		X
5. ... when it all seemed ...	X	
6. ... had the government decided ...		X
7. ... you got home.		X

1. « Tu es paresseux, bête et personne ne t'aime. » Imagine ce que cela te ferait si ton meilleur ami te parlait comme ça.
2. Est-ce qu'il t'arrive de regretter de ne pas être plus séduisant ou plus intelligent ?
3. Depuis quand n'as-tu pas entendu une remarque flatteuse ?
4. Imagine que tu échoues à ton permis de conduire ! Tu ferais quoi ?
5. Il fut un temps où les choses semblaient beaucoup plus faciles à faire.
6. Imagine l'indignation dans l'opinion si le gouvernement avait décidé de modifier sa politique !
7. Peut-être vaut-il mieux attendre que tu arrives chez toi ?

P. 63 Exercice niveau 1
2. 1. *I wish she were prettier.*
    2. *I wish he were not so old.*
    3. *If I were you, I would talk to them.*
    4. *I wish I had the time to visit them.*
    5. *I wish you were more supportive.*

P. 65 Exercice niveau 1
2. 1. *"I wish I were with you."*
       J'aimerais être avec toi. / Je regrette de ne pas être avec toi.
    2 *"I wish you were not so childish!"*
       J'aimerais que tu sois un peu moins puéril.
    3. *"I wish you would stop complaining."*
       J'aimerais que tu arrêtes de te plaindre.
    4. *"I wish I were back there."*
       J'aimerais être là-bas à nouveau. / Je regrette de ne pas être là-bas à nouveau.
    Exercice niveau 2
3. 1. *I wish I could get in touch with him.*
       Je regrette de ne pas pouvoir le contacter.
    2. *I wish you would tell him the truth.*
       J'aimerais que tu lui dises la vérité.
    3. *He behaves as if he were not there.*
       Il se comporte comme s'il n'était pas là.
    4. *I wish she would stop playing her music.*
       J'aimerais qu'elle arrête sa musique.
    5. *I wish I hadn't missed such a fantastic opportunity.*
       Je regrette d'avoir manqué une occasion pareille !
    6. *I wish he hadn't failed.*
       Je regrette qu'il ait échoué.

1.

1	2	3	4	5	6
a	c	d	f	b	e

Exercice niveau 2

3. 1. *I wish he could have come.*
   2. *It's about time you made up your mind.*
   3. *If he had been told the truth, he would have come at once.*
   4. *I wish you would leave me alone.*
   5. *I wish I could have done it myself.*

P. 71 Exercice niveau 1

1. 1. *You must listen to me!* Tu dois m'écouter !
   2. *I simply can't speak German.*
      Je ne parle tout simplement pas allemand.
   3. *I think that you should think it over.* Je pense que tu devrais y réfléchir.
   4. *He may stay as long as he wishes.* Il peut rester autant qu'il veut.
   5. *You certainly needn't see him twice a week.*
      Tu n'as certainement pas besoin de le voir deux fois par semaine.
   6. *Shall I give you a hand?* Je te donne (tu veux) un coup de main ?
   7. *He can't be back!* Il est impossible qu'il soit rentré !
   8. *It may be true.* C'est peut-être vrai.

Exercice niveau 2

2.

	Capacité ou incapacité	
	dans le passé	*imaginée ou envisagée*
1. *Could you help me if I asked you?* Tu pourrais m'aider si je te le demandais ?		X
2. *I couldn't help it! It was so funny!* Je n'ai pas pu m'en empêcher. C'était si drôle !	X	
3. *I wish I could stay.* J'aimerais pouvoir rester.		X
4. *I couldn't get in touch with you.* *That's why I was worried.* Je ne pouvais pas te contacter. C'est pour ça que j'étais inquiet.	X	
5. *If only she could help me!* Si seulement elle pouvait m'aider !		X

P. 73 Exercice niveau 2

1. 1. *You **should** try to talk to her.*
   2. *He **won't** leave her.*
   3. *He **would** go out at night*
   4. *You **shouldn't have** left her!*
   5. *You **needn't** stay.*
   6. *You **should have** said something.*

P. 75 Exercice niveau 1

1. 1. *You will have an excellent working environment and two weeks' vacation.*
   2. *You needn't have child care experience.*
   3. *You can start any time.*
   4. *You must be aged 18 to 26.*
   5. *You can either work full-time or part-time.*
   6. *You shouldn't wait too long.*

   Exercices niveau 2

2. *"You **must** come to dinner. We want to get to know you better."*
   "Actually, I'm not going out much in the evenings just at present. I'm not feeling very well."
   *"You **mustn't** give in, you know, you **must** make an effort. Is there any reason why you **can't** come?"*

3. *"You **must** come round one of these days."*
   *"**Need** I tell you again how much I miss you?"*
   *"No, you **needn't** tell me what I already know."*
   *"I **must** say I was surprised to hear that you had moved so quickly."*
   *"You **must** try to understand me."*

P. 77 Exercice niveau 1

2. 1. *Ask him who he is, **will** you?*
   2. *Can you stop here? **I'll** give him a ring.*
   3. *I **would** be very unhappy if it was true.*
   4. *It's too hot. **I'll** open the window.*
   5. *Don't worry. It **won't** take long.*
   6. *No, thank you. **I'll** have a drink later.*

   Exercice niveau 2

4. 1. *"Oh, yes, he **would**."*
   2. *You **might** have helped him!*
   3. *Is there any reason why you **can't** come? Or **won't** you come?*
   4. *He **won't** answer.*
   5. ***Shall** we stay?*

P. 79 Exercice niveau 1

2. *She picked up the phone and dialled his number.*
   *"Leon! I've got the most extraordinary thing in my garden! A big blue van! What **should** I do?"*
   *"I think you **should** go and ask the driver what he's doing there. Maybe he's just stopped for lunch."*
   *"He **can't** have lunch in my garden! That's impossible! Maybe I **should** call the police," said Anna.*
   *"I don't think it **will** be necessary. He'**ll** probably be off by the time they arrive. You **needn't** worry," said Leon reassuringly.*

   Exercice niveau 2

4. 1. *You needn't tell them. They needn't know what you've done. What would happen if they were to find out (if they found out) the truth ?*
   2. *Remember that you mustn't see them again or try to talk to them. You must try to forget what happened.*
   3. *You can't understand. If you knew the truth, you wouldn't be here.*
   4. *He should be more careful. He can't swim.*

P. 81 Exercice niveau 2
2. 1. He suggested that I *should go (I go) away*.
    2. It is unfair that he *should be punished*.
    3. She suggested that they *should go (they go) with them*.
    4. It was getting late. I suggested *going*.

P. 83 Exercice niveau 1
2. 1. "You *mustn't* go on. I won't allow you to go any further."
    2. "You *don't have to* answer if you don't want to."
    3. "No parking." Visitors *mustn't* park here.
    4. It's free access. We *don't have to* pay.
    5. There's no need to hurry. We *don't have to* be there before lunch.
    Exercice niveau 2
4. 1. He came home. I didn't have to phone him.
    2. Can he go now? He needn't stay. / He doesn't have to stay.
    3. We couldn't let them go. We had to ask them to stay.
    4. You mustn't see them again ! I don't want you to talk to them.
    5. I don't think we'll be allowed to talk to him.

P. 85 Exercice niveau 1
2. 1. You must be right.
    2. He may be late.
    2. You must go before he comes back.
    3. He must be looking for you.
    4. She may be thinking of him.
    Exercice niveau 2
4. 1. They must be having a row. Fait présent
    2. You must have read the whole book by 6 o'clock. Fait futur
    3. She should be back by 7 o'clock, logically. Fait futur
    4. She may speak to you when it's over. Fait futur
    5. I must have lost it in the park. Fait passé
    6. She may not know what happened. Fait présent

P. 87 Exercice niveau 1
1. 1. a) Peut-être est-il marié.
    2. c) Il va peut-être changer d'avis.
    3. a) Peut-être ne le sait-il pas encore.
    4. c) Ils doivent être en train d'essayer de trouver une solution.
    5. b) Elle pourrait bien arriver d'une minute à l'autre.
    6. a) Elle doit certainement lui avoir parlé.
    Exercice niveau 2
2. 1. She still felt very excited. Maybe it was the wine, or something else.
       "Charles *may be phoning* Alice at this very moment," she thought.
    2. Are you thirsty? This little café must *be* quite expensive but maybe
       we could *order* a glass of wine or something.
    3. I regret missing that exhibition. It must *have been* quite interesting.
    4. "I've ordered three bottles of champagne."
       "What? You *must be joking!*"
    5. I can't *believe* it! You can't *have lost* my diamond ring!

P. 89 Exercice niveau 1
2. *In hospital*
   1. "He must be five or six years old."
   2. "He may be too distressed to talk."
   3. "His arm must be broken."
   4. "His parents must be looking for him."
   5. "He may have been kidnapped."
   6. "The driver may have run away after the accident."

Exercice niveau 2
3. 1. He must be wondering where we are.
   2. He may call me tonight.
   3. He may not love her.
   4. She might well be the one we're looking for.
   5. She may have forgotten.

P. 91 Exercice niveau 1
2. 1. It must be over now.
   2. She can't know him.
   3. She may not want to talk to you.
   4. He may be phoning her.
   5. The police may have found the murderer.

Exercice niveau 2
4. 1. He must have paid a lot for this house.
   2. He can't have won.
   3. They may have chosen the right one.
   4. He must have left fairly recently.
   5. He must be having a shower.
   6. He must have been having lunch.
   7. They may not have seen him.
   8. He may be obliged to resign.

P. 93 Exercices niveau 2
2. "Did you go to Vienna with your brother?"
   "No, I didn't. I suppose I **could have gone** with him but it didn't seem to be the right time for me."
   "Why didn't you phone? We **could have arranged** something for you. I think you need a holiday. Have you got friends you **could stay** with?"
   "Yes, I have a dear friend in Paris. Perhaps I **could go** there."
3. 1. b) Do you need
   2. a) have been
   3. b) didn't need to
   4. c) needn't have

CHAPITRE 5

P. 95 Exercice niveau I

2. 1. He**'ll** be back on Sunday.
Repère futur **>** *will.*
2. It's dark. I**'ll** turn on the light.
Acte logiquement attendu **>** *will.*
3. They**'re going to** get married.
Pas de repère temporel **>** *be going to.*
4. I**'ll** go with them if you ask me to.
Subordonnée en *if* **>** *will.*
5. Kevin: "There's a man waiting for you."
Sarah: "I**'ll** go and ask him who he is."
Acte logiquement attendu.
6. We**'ll** find a solution sooner or later.
Repère temporel **>** *will.*

P. 97 Exercice niveau I

1. 1. a) 'll
2. a) won't
3. c) 'll
4. c) 'm going to

Exercices niveau 2

2. **Libra**
Your troubles are just temporary and **will last** only while Venus **is** in your sign.
Scorpio
When **will you finally agree** to settle down? This is a great time to tell your partner what you **have** in mind for the future.
Sagittarius
This week **will bring** you a letter from an old friend. Try to **get** in touch with him/her as soon as you get the letter.
Capricorn
You may be keen to get some work done but you**'ll find** it hard to achieve much until your sweetheart **gets** in touch with you.
Aquarius
Any social activities at the weekend **will go** well as long as you **make** an effort to be cheerful.
Pisces
When **will you stop** worrying? If you seek out friends outside your immediate circle, you**'ll feel better**.
Aries
Your nerves **will be stretched** this week as there is so much going on. The situation **will improve** as soon as Venus **enters** your sign.

3. 1. I'll leave when he comes back.
2. I won't see him until he calls me.
3. I'll be with them when she arrives.
4. I'll tell you as soon as I know.

CHAPITRE 6

P. 99 Exercice niveau 1
2. 1. There **are** some people in the hall.
   2. My luggage **is** too heavy.
   3. There **is** no furniture in the guestroom.
   4. The news **is** quite interesting today.
   5. Her hair **is** long and very thick.
   6. The police **are** looking for a tall, dark-haired man.
   7. Business **is** business.

Exercice niveau 2
4. **Gemini**
   There were **times** when you were locked in **difficulties**. Don't worry! The next few **days** will bring **happiness** into your life.
   Sagittarius
   You need some **advice**. Remember that **time** is **money**.
   Leo
   Do not provide your **enemies** with unnecessary **information**.

P. 101 Exercice niveau 1
2. 1. b) plenty of
   2. b) some
   3. b) a loaf of
   4. a) ø
   5. b) a
   6. a) ø

Exercices niveau 2
3. 1. **Several pieces** of furniture were stolen yesterday.
   2. Here is **a piece of** advice for you!
   3. He's made ø good progress lately.
   4. He was not able to give me **the piece** of information I wanted.
4. 1. b) ø
   2. b) was no
   3. b) some
   4. a) a lot of

P. 103 Exercice niveau 1
1. 1. a) like
   2. a) is blocking
   3. a) are
   4. b) is
   5. b) is too much
   6. b) are
   7. a) is
   8. b) is
   9. a) is

2. 1. *The police arrested him, didn't **they**?*
   2. *The United States will fight terrorism, won't **it**?*
   3. *Nobody phoned, did **they**?*
   4. *The progress made truly surprised them, didn't **it**?*
   5. *The French fought for them, didn't **they**?*
   6. *The sheep gathered in the field, didn't **they**?*
   7. *The news came in late, didn't **it**?*
   8. *Their advice astounded you, didn't **it**?*
   9. *The rubbish will be disposed of, won't **it**?*

CHAPITRE 7

P. 107 Exercices niveau 2
2. ***The** Prime Minister has announced **a** 15 per cent pay rise for ø Britain's 470,000 nurses. He said on Thursday that **the** wage increases for ø nurses and doctors would cost **the** government **an** extra £750 million. **The** news was announced to **the** public on ø February 10th.*
3. *ø Spanish women are having ø fewer babies, according to **a** recent government study. **The** birth rate dropped from 2.9 children per family in 1974 to 1.7 in 1994. **The** rate required to replace **the** population is 2.1 children per ø family. **The** decline in ø Spain reflects trends elsewhere in ø Western Europe.*

P. 109 Exercice niveau 1
1. 1. *Time to go to ø bed, children!*
   2. *The hospital is near **the** church.*
   3. *Careful! Men at ø work.*
   4. *"Aren't you going to be late?" "I don't know, what is **the** time?"*
   5. *Go as far as **the** market, then turn right.*
   6. *There is no place like ø home.*
   7. *Would you like to go to **the** pictures with me?*
   Exercice niveau 2
3. *ø Thousands of ø young victims of ø school bullies were given some new hope yesterday. **The** problem is so severe that it drives many children to ø suicide. **The** government announced two measures aimed at stopping **the** torment. ø Free leaflets will be available for **the** start of **the** autumn term. They will tell ø teachers, ø parents and ø pupils how to develop **an** anti-bullying programme to tackle **the** scandal. During **the** summer two Department of Education films will be screened on ø TV dramatising **the** problem and urging ø **(the)** victims not to suffer in ø silence. **The** programme follows some research showing that ø bullied children never report their anguish to ø teachers.*

P. 111   Exercice niveau 1
2.   1. c) the film
      2. a) President
      3. c) the problem ... unemployment
      4. a) Astronomers ... a new solar system
     Exercice niveau 2
4.   ø Trains want to challenge ø airlines by offering **the** same facilities.
     ø Films and ø video games will be available on ø British Rail trains from
     ø next month.
     ø Travellers will have **the** opportunity to hire **a** portable video player and
     watch **the** films and ø computer games they have chosen from **a** library
     of 12 different movies.

P. 113   Exercices niveau 1
1.   1. a) air ... water
      2. c) large areas ... radioactive waste
      3. c) The use ... drugs
      4. b) a
2.   In Springfield, Oregon, last May, **a** teenager carrying **a** gun shot 22 students
     and killed two. **The** number of ø murders in ø American schools has
     increased tremendously. Some experts say that the number of ø shootings
     could be reduced by making ø access to ø guns more difficult. ø Teenagers
     should not be allowed to carry ø guns in any situation. But ø gun-control
     seems to be one of **the** most difficult things to achieve in ø American schools.
     Exercice niveau 2
3.   1. Perhaps **the** American Dream will never again flourish on this planet.
      2. And to restore it, we have to capture **the** spirit that exemplified it
          - **the** spirit of ø individualism, of ø self reliance, of ø risk taking - **the**
          spirit described by Rose Wilder Lane in Give Me Liberty.
      3. ø Freedom and ø equality cannot coexist. We have tried it, like others
          before us who attempted it. **The** results have been disastrous.
      4. **The** sooner we admit our errors and begin accepting our punishment, **the**
          sooner we can get back to enjoying **the** freedom that has escaped us.
      5. Ultimately, ø freedom must be achieved or it must be lost in its pursuit.
          From Restoring the American Dream by R.J. Ringer.

P. 115   Exercice niveau 1
2.   Should ø private companies be allowed to advertise in ø schools? Patrick is
     a teacher in California. He says ø advertising should be banned from ø
     schools. He thinks that ø education and ø advertising are incompatible.
     Some American schools use ø advertising to solve ø budget problems.
     Exercice niveau 2
4.   According to ø aid workers in Africa, ø thousands of people are dying of ø
     disease and ø starvation. In some places ø people lie dead where they have
     collapsed through ø dysentery or lack of ø water. ø Orphaned children
     struggle to survive without the basic supplies. ø Aid agencies are now calling
     on ø British people to help them launch **an** urgent relief operation.

P. 117 Exercices niveau 1

1. 1. This table is made of ø wood.
   2. Have you met Mr Higgins, **the** chairman of our association?
   3. When he heard ø Professor George lecturing, he became very interested in ø physics.
   4. **The** effects of ø technical change can sometimes lead to ø deterioration in **the** natural environment and in **the** quality of ø life.

2. **A** 22-year-old artist has asked some of **the** most famous people in **the** world to join in **the** fight against ø anti-personnel landmines. ø Princess Diana did a lot against ø landmines. Her work has helped ø artists to understand the problem. Brian, 22, is a painter. He says: "I understand what ø life must be like when you have lost your hand or foot." He has asked other artists to contribute to **the** book against ø landmines. According to **the** Red Cross, there are ø millions of mines around **the** world waiting to explode.

Exercices niveau 2

3. Scotland Yard confirmed yesterday that ø detectives were investigating **a** burglary at **the** consulting rooms of **a** doctor who treated the Princess of Wales for ø eating disorder. **The** thief entered **the** rooms of ø Dr L., **the** therapist **the** Princess of Wales is known to have consulted over problems with bulimia nervosa and slimmers' disease. **The** thief stole **the** computer containing **the** Princess's ø medical records, with intimate details of her health and personal traumas.

4. 1. c) a horrible meeting
   2. b) nice they were
   3. b) a pity
   4. b) nice these flowers are

CHAPITRE 8

P. 119 Exercice niveau 1
2. 1. **Your parents' house** is too small for you now.
   2. **John's car** is parked out there.
   3. **Our company's new manager** has won the prize.
   4. **The government's foreign policy** is risky.
   5. **After the children's departure**, he flew to Sweden.
   Exercice niveau 2
4. 1. It is **the city's busiest place**.
   2. **Yesterday's events** have caused a disaster.
   3. **The president's** speech was inappropriate.
   4. **The country's representatives** have decided to vote against him.
   5. He returned home after **a week's holiday** in Spain.
   6. **After two hours' walking**, they were exhausted.
   7. **The town's only big store** has closed down.
   8. This is **Ken Loach's best film**.

P. 121 Exercices niveau 1
1. 1. c) Whose … yours
   2. c) of mine
   3. b) of yours
   4. c) theirs
   5. c) the boys' room
2. 1. This is my mother's computer.
   2. Where are your brother's clothes?
   3. Claire is gone. She's left her car in the garage.
   4. He is a friend of mine.
   5. Yesterday's film was much better.
   6. These keys are not mine. Whose are they?
   Exercices niveau 2
3. 1. b) two years' sentence
   2. b) actress's
   3. c) of her own
   4. c) two weeks'
   5. a) a week's
4. 1. Don't be an idiot! Nobody wants to kill you, why should **they**?
   2. Everybody came in **their** car.
   3. They both got nice presents; Peter was very happy with **his** but his sister didn't like **hers**.
   4. I only borrowed it, it's not **mine**.
   5. Having a room of **one**'s own is a legitimate claim.

CHAPITRE 9

P. 123 Exercice niveau I

2. 1. I'm seeing **some** friends of mine tonight.
2. Are there **any** words you don't understand?
3. I'd like **some** more wine.
4. He feels very lonely. He has **no** friends there.
5. Have you had **any** messages from him?

Exercice niveau 2

4. 1. Haven't you got **any** money for this?
2. No, thanks, I don't want **a** drink now.
3. I couldn't buy him **a** ticket because I had **no** money at all.
4. Have you had **any** news from her? Did you send her **a** birthday card?
5. If there are **any** messages for me, please forward them to my office.
6. I was surprised to see that he had **no** luggage at all.
7. Some people say it's **no** use trying.
8. I haven't had **any** help from them.
9. She hasn't got **a** job and she hasn't had **any** advice from them.

P. 125 Exercices niveau I

2. 1. Would you like **some** more fruit?
2. He hates socializing, so he has very **few** friends.
3. There is **not much** coffee left. You'll have to make **some**.
4. There aren't **many** people around.
5. I know very little French.

3. 1. **Lots** of young actors dream of becoming movie stars. Very **few** succeed.
2. How **many** actors do you know?
3. Only very **few** stars can guarantee a movie's success; in fact there are only three of them: Tom Cruise, George Clooney and Tom Hanks.
4. How **much** money do they earn in the movie business?

P. 127 Exercice niveau I

1. 1. **Most** people said they tried to quit once.
2. Very **few** smokers said they were influenced by other smokers.
3. **Some** people said they were afraid of putting on weight if they stopped smoking.
4. **Half (of)** the people who were interviewed said that they found it too difficult to stop.

3. **Exercice niveau 2**

   *In many developing countries millions of children die from malnutrition. **Most of** the people who live there work 14 or 16 hours per day. They live in **the most** dreadful conditions. For **most of** the year they go hungry. **The most** terrible thing is that they have no opportunity to make their lives better. You could help them by sponsoring a child. It costs no more than £12 a month. To us, that's nothing. But to a child and family in a poor village, it can be **the most** valuable thing. Your sponsorship can give them **most of** the things they need.*

P. 129 Exercice niveau 1

2. 1. *a) All*
   2. *b) Most*
   3. *a) thousand*
   4. *a) little*
   5. *b) too many*

   Exercice niveau 2

3. 1. *The US seems to generate **more** jobs than Germany and France. There are **fewer** unemployed people in the US than in **any** European country.*
   2. *American specialists say that there aren't **many** signs of recovery for either France or Germany. They have **little** confidence that the situation will improve in the near future. They say that **no** jobs will be created until economic growth gets back to 3 or 4 per cent. There is **much** concern over Italy too, which does not seem to be doing any better than its European partners.*

CHAPITRE 10

P. 131 Exercice niveau 1

2.

	Alan	Nora	Autre(s) (précisez)
1. *I had...*		X	
2. *I'm glad.*	X		
3. *...enjoyed **yourself**...*		X	
4. *...didn't **you**?*		X	
5. *...besides **you**...*		X	
6. ***We** talked...*			Nora, Elaine, Paul
7. ***They** hadn't spoken...*			Elaine, Paul
8. *...to **each other**...*			Elaine, Paul
9. *...did **they**?*			Somebody, other people

P. 133 Exercice niveau 1
- 2. 1. c) Me
  2. b) they ... them
  3. b) himself
  4. a) There
  5. c) there ... no one

Exercices niveau 2
- 4. 1. Don't you know that Paul Ross now lives by **himself**?
  2. It's not your fault. You can't blame **yourself**.
  3. Helen and Paul never speak to **each other**.
  4. Everybody liked the film, didn't **they**?
- 5. 1. a) one
  2. a) one
  3. c) yourself
  4. c) each other ... ø
  5. a) There

P. 135 Exercice niveau 1
- 2. 1. He wants something but I have nothing for him (to give him).
  2. He knows nothing.
  3. Someone saw him with her.
  4. No one knows her.
  5. There's nothing to do. There's no one to talk to.

Exercice niveau 2
- 4. **Italy**
  10 & 18 days from £89 pounds only!
  Nowhere can you find **anything** cheaper!
  Price includes excellent guided tours to **all** the places you've always dreamed of: Venice, Rome, Florence. Top hotels with pools. **All** rooms with private facilities. Phone now for brochure. Only **a few** places left!

CHAPITRE 11

P. 137 Exercice niveau 1
- 2. 1. He was a silly young boy.
  2. We had a lovely long walk along the beach.
  3. It was a good old American thriller.
  4. She was wearing red leather sandals.
  5. She was a dark-eyed Spanish girl.
  6. He had a big black German motorbike.

Exercice niveau 2
- 4. 1. Most of **the** homeless people I know have never had a chance of starting a real job.
  2. ø Jobs have become scarce for **the** over-fifties.
  3. **The** unemployed have created an association.
  4. There are more and more retired **people** in Northern Europe.
  5. The local authorities do not do much to help **the** city's homeless. There are more and more homeless **people** in the town centre.

CHAPITRE 12

P. 139 Exercice niveau 1

2. 1. Lots of children (a great number of children) have better results when the school year is longer.
2. Some teachers think that children do better work when the summer break is shorter.
3. Some children are just as tired in September.
4. Their results are worse than in June.

P. 141 Exercice niveau 2

1. 1. France has **the lowest** inflation rate. However, French interest rates are **higher than** in Germany or in the UK. Unemployment in France is still much **lower than** in Spain, though it is **higher than** in Germany. Inflation is not **so high** in Germany **as** in Italy or Spain, though it is **higher than** in the UK.
2. The situation in Spain is **worse than** anywhere else in Europe. France, Germany and the UK have **the best** unemployment rates.
3. The UK seems to be doing a bit **better than** France and Italy in the field of unemployment. Inflation is **lower than** in Italy, Germany or Spain, though it is not **so low as** in France. The UK has **the lowest** interest rates in Europe.

P. 143 Exercice niveau 1

2. 1. She looks much **better** now!
2. Don't worry. It is **less serious** than we thought.
3. He is the **younger** of the two.
4. You'd better ask for **further** information.
5. She's not **so (as) pretty** as she used to be.
6. What a good film! Far **more interesting** than the other one!
7. All the dresses fitted her, so she bought **the least** expensive one. She had to be careful with her money.

Exercice niveau 2

3. A recent report states that girls are closing the gap in maths and science. What's more, they are now doing **as well as**, and in some cases **better than** boys at A-level. The academic gap between the sexes appears at around the age of seven and has become marked by secondary school: girls tend to work **more carefully than** boys, are distracted **less easily** and produce **neater** work. While boys prefer to play football or a computer game in their free time, girls are **more likely** to read or talk to their friends or parents, so improving their literary skills. Many teachers find that the boys have **lower** reading skills at 11 than the girls. Adapted from The Independent, July 28, 1994.

P. 145 Exercice niveau 1

2. 1. He made his letter **longer** by a few lines.
2. Their situation is **getting better**.
3. Your decision makes success **more likely**.

Exercice niveau 2

3. b - Food in Greece is much **cheaper** than anywhere else. In fact, the Greek Islands seem to be **the cheapest** place for food. The price of food is **much higher** in Florida and the Canary Islands **than** in Spain or Tunisia.
- The Greek Islands offer **better** prices **than** all the other places. A week in Greece is even **less expensive than** a week in Malta. But Italy is **the best place** for wine-drinkers. Florida is **far more expensive than** any other place.

CHAPITRE 13

P. 149 Exercice niveau 1

2. It is late **afternoon** but it is still very hot. The boys are playing **volley-ball**. But it is so hot that Edith can't even think of joining them. Most of the girls are lying in the sun. They are **sunbathing** in their bikinis. Edith is wearing a white **sweat-shirt** and she also has her **sun-glasses** on to protect her eyes against the blazing sun. Next to her, a **teenager** with a **walkman** is listening to a new tape.

Exercices niveau 2

4. 1. I've seen the brown-eyed girl.
   2. He is a funny-looking boy.
   3. She is a dark-skinned girl.
   4. He is a dangerous-looking man.
   5. The doctor was a fifty-five-year-old man.

5.

1. What does he / it do? What's his / her job?	**Scriptwriter** : he writes scripts - Scénariste racing driver : a driver involved in racing Coureur automobile
2. What is it for?	**safety screen** : a screen for safety Ecran de protection
3. What sort of?	**Gunshots** : shots fired from gun Coups de feu **a brick wall** : a wall made of bricks Mur de brique **heart attack** : attack of the heart Crise cardiaque **war games** : games with battles in them Jeux de guerre
4. B = A. identité	**girl-friend** : his friend is a girl
5. Activité	

P. 151 Exercice niveau 1

2. 1. He was very **friendly** with us.
   2. He's been very **successful**.
   3. She was the most **attractive** woman I had ever seen.
   4. Don't worry. This operation is quite **painless**.
   5. My other friends were less **enthusiastic** about Arthur.
   6. There is nothing we can do; we are quite **helpless**.

Exercices niveau 2

5. 1. Being **jobless** is worse than anything else. **Joblessness** has become a nation-wide problem. The number of available **jobs** is falling everyday. The **jobless** and the **homeless** are deprived of any real support.
   2. **Homelessness** and **joblessness** are related problems. Being **homeless** makes it impossible for anyone to get a decent **job**.

6. 1. The sleeves are too long. Have them **shortened**!
   2. Be careful. The fog is **thickening**.
   3. Stop that music! It is **deafening**!
   4. When she heard the news her face **brightened**.

CHAPITRE 14

P. 153 Exercice niveau 1

2. *I don't like running. Cycling is more pleasant. My sister loves skiing but I don't. My brother likes tennis-playing very much. But tennis-playing is really too tiring ! Swimming is boring. I've never tried rock-climbing. But it's probably too risky. In fact, what I like best is dancing.*
Exercice niveau 2

4. 1. *Hadn't you better **send for** the doctor?*
   2. *You've got **to send for** the doctor right now.*
   3. *I'd rather **tell** my parents before we do anything.*
   4. *I'd prefer **to ask** my parents first.*
   5. *I'd prefer **to go** alone rather than stay with them.*
   6. *What do you want me **to do**? **Go**?*

P. 155 Exercice niveau 1

2. *I'm 18. My parents would like me **to go** to university but I don't like the idea. I'd rather **do** something different. I'm determined **to show** my family that I intend **to have** a career. I've always wanted **to be** a model. I've already sent a few photos of myself to an agency in London and they've told me **to go and see them**. But I live in a far-off town and I can't afford **to travel** to London. Can you **help** me?*
Exercice niveau 2

4. 1. ***You'd love to see him again**, wouldn't you?*
   2. ***He was busy working** when I phoned.*
   3. *I hope **he won't forget to phone me** as soon as he arrives.*
   4. *How does she put up with him?*
      ***She is the only one to find him interesting**!*
   5. ***I loved talking** to you last night.*

P. 157 Exercice niveau 1

2. *Grace Whitney, a beautiful 28-year-old girl, started boxing 18 months ago. "People are so negative," she complains. "I want **to prove** that a woman's place is in the ring. **Boxing** is a skill. You have **to be** quick, fit and strong. You have **to train** long and hard. Every week, I spend hours **training** in the gym. There is an enormous difference between **boxing** and violence. I'm not saying that **boxing** is totally safe. But men and women shouldn't **be** treated differently."*
Exercice niveau 2

4. 1. *She suggested giving him a ring.*
   2. *She admitted killing him.*
   3. *She denied talking to Jim.*
   4. *She said she regretted hurting her.*

P. 159 Exercices niveau 2

3. 1. *She was blamed for **going out** at night.*
   2. *Can't you understand that I did it **to help** you?*
   3. *He came back without his wife **realizing** it.*
   4. *The roads used **to be** dangerous but the situation has improved.*
   5. *I'm not used **to driving**.*
   6. *We'll have to wait for them **to give** an answer.*

4. *Gillian Anderson, who plays the part of Agent Scully in the X Files studied* **acting** *at college in Chicago and graduated in 1990. This led her* **to move** *to Los Angeles. But she had no connections and no money. So she had* **to work** *in a restaurant for a couple of months. Then she got the job in the X Files. "I'm very unlike Scully," says Gillian." Scully never complains of* **being stressed**. *She is used* **to working** *long hours. She doesn't worry about* **looking** *fat. She appears* **to have** *no insecurities. She devotes all her time to* **being** *Agent Scully."*

P. 161 Exercice niveau 1
2.

1	2	3	4
b	c	d	a

Exercices niveau 2
4. 1. *Look! It's beginning* **to rain**!
   2. *They couldn't help* **laughing** *whenever the teacher stopped watching them.*
   3. *The kitchen wants* **painting**.
   4. *The children were busy* **writing** *on the walls with felt-tipped pens.*
   5. *Do you really need* **to tell** *them she's gone?*
   6. *I resented* **being** *treated like a child.*
   7. *He avoided* **meeting** *her.*
   8. *I regret* **buying** *that old car. It was a mistake.*
   9. *Can't you give up* **smoking** *for a while?*
   10. *He didn't feel like* **coming**.
   11. *He kept* **saying** *that he wasn't guilty.*
   12. *This is really worth* **trying**.
5. *I've made arrangements for someone* **to be** *with you. You can't* **be** *left alone like this. I telephoned Paula. Well, she's got nothing* **to do** *all day, and she could* **get** *you a bit of shopping. You'd better* **eat** *something now. And stop* **complaining**, *please!*

P. 163 Exercices niveau 2
3. 1. *The last time I saw them, she seemed* **to be** *in love with him.*
   2. *Paul Twiggy, the snooker player, narrowly escaped jail after* **refusing to appear** *in court for a drink-drive offence.*
   3. *He is said* **to have died** *of a heart attack on the very night they came back.*
   4. *She is supposed* **to be** *in Italy right now.*
   5. *They are looking for the woman who is believed* **to have placed** *a bomb outside the embassy, yesterday.*
   6. *One of the most famous football players has been forbidden* **to take part** *in the World Cup after being accused of* **taking** *drugs.*
4. 1. *He is said to have disappeared overnight.*
   2. *She is believed to have lost it two weeks ago.*
   3. *He was said to be the culprit.*
   4. *He was thought to have been killed two days before.*
   5. *It was reported to have taken place there.*

P. 165 Exercice niveau I
1. 1. b) them to come
    2. a) you talking
    3. c) used to
    4. b) going
    5. c) not say
    6. c) you to give
    7. b) to working
    Exercices niveau 2
3. 1. Do you mind me (my) calling you tonight?
    2. He expected her to obey.
    3. I can't stand your interrupting me all the time.
    4. Do you object to my (me) going out?
    5. They told us not to say anything.
4. 1. I remember talking to her the other night.
    2. It's worth trying.
    3. I look forward to your meeting them.
    4. She avoids talking to them.
    5. He doesn't mind his sister leaving.

CHAPITRE 15

Exercice niveau 1

2. *1. He advised me to run away.*
2. He didn't expect them to pass.
3. He ordered them to put up their hands.
4. He asked us to open the door.
5. He told her to sit down.
Exercice niveau 2

4. *When I met Ann she said she wanted **me to look after her children**. It was a risky adventure because **her children were (are) unmanageable**. Ann calmly advised **me to be firm with them**. She said that **they were extremely unstable**. She told **me never to give in to their freaks**. But the reality was far beyond my expectations. The first time I asked **them to get ready for a walk**, they ran off shrieking. When I told **them to sit down** for lunch, they tore up their napkins. Needless to say they wouldn't watch television for more than ten minutes on end. They simply refused to obey me. In the end they **made me cry**. I was ashamed and desperate and angry.*

P. 169 Exercice niveau 1

2. *1. It's hard for her to bring up her children alone.*
2. This money is for you to buy something nice.
3. I find it difficult to understand you.
4. It's time for you to go.
5. He was said to be in Germany.
Exercice niveau 2

4. *1. They did it for everyone to see them.*
Ils l'ont fait pour que tout le monde les voie.
2. He was blamed for not saying where he'd been.
On lui a reproché de ne pas avoir dit où il était allé.
3. He was punished for stealing the money.
On l'a puni pour avoir volé l'argent.
4. I thank you for not letting me down when I needed you.
Je te remercie de ne pas m'avoir laissé tomber lorsque j'ai eu besoin de toi.
5. He'll long be remembered for being cruel.
On se souviendra longtemps de lui en raison de sa cruauté.

CHAPITRE 16

P. 171 Exercice niveau 2

3. 1. *I had it **changed** at the garage yesterday.*
      Je l'ai fait changer au garage hier.
   2. *I'm exhausted! The gym teacher made us **run** for one hour non-stop.*
      Je suis épuisée. Le prof de gym nous a fait courir pendant un heure sans interruption.
   3. *My hair is too dark. I'll have it **dyed**.*
      Mes cheveux sont trop foncés. Je vais les faire teindre.
   4. *When I came back from Russia, the customs officers made me **open** my cases.*
      Quand je suis revenue de Russie, les douaniers m'ont fait ouvrir mes valises.
   5. *I eventually made him **talk** about his childhood.*
      J'ai fini par le faire parler de son enfance.
   6. *They made us **understand** that we were to leave as soon as possible.*
      Ils nous ont fait comprendre qu'ils devaient partir dès que possible.
   7. *I've just had the kitchen **painted**.*
      Je viens de faire repeindre la cuisine.

P. 173 Exercice niveau 1

3. 1. *I made them laugh.*
   2. *They made me go out.*
   3. *I've had my hair cut.*
   4. *They had the computer repaired.*

Exercices niveau 2

6. 1. *I had the wheel changed.* J'ai fait changer la roue.
   2. *They made me clean the room.* Ils m'ont fait nettoyer la pièce.
   3. *I had it shortened.* Je l'ai fait raccourcir.
   4. *We made them write their names on the book.*
      Nous leur avons fait écrire leur nom sur le livre.
   5. *She made me cry.* Elle m'a fait pleurer.
   6. *I had some photographs taken.* J'ai fait faire des photos.

7. 1. *He made them lie.*
   2. *I had this (that) text translated.*
   3. *They made me believe it was true.*
   4. *He had some wine brought in.*
   5. *I let them go on.*

CHAPITRE 17

P. 175 Exercice niveau 1

2. 1. *The man who had an accident in Keswick lives in London.*
   2. *The girl who was taken to hospital works in Lancaster.*
   3. *The accident that happened here was caused by two German tourists.*
   4. *The boy who came first is my brother.*

   Exercice niveau 2

4. 1. *Tell me everything ø you can remember.*
   2. *This is the house **that** belonged to Paul Jones.*
   3. *I've bought the car ø we saw in Leicester Square.*
   4. *This is the person ø I wanted you to meet.*
   5. *This is the best thing **that** ever happened to me.*
   6. *Don't look at the mess ø we've made.*

P. 177 Exercice niveau 1

2. 1. *I came across an article about a boy **whose** photo was on the front page.*
   2. *He was the boy **who** invented that funny video game.*
   3. *It's the best game ø I've ever tested! It's the only game that doesn't leave you frustrated.*
   4. *My brother, **who** is very fond of all multi-media materials, read the article too.*
   5. *He said it was the most interesting thing ø he had ever read.*

   Exercices niveau 2

5. 1. *This is **what** I like best about him.*
   2. *The problem ø they'll have to deal with is very serious.*
   3. *He's the last person ø I saw.*
   4. *This is **what** I remember best.*
   5. *This is the only house **that** has a balcony.*

6. 1. *He spoke about the bag ø I had left in the hall.*
   2. *He called the police immediately, **which** was the best thing to do.*
   3. *The man ø I introduced to you is a lawyer.*
   4. *I put it back in the refrigerator, **which** was silly of me.*
   5. *Tell me the names of the students **whose** results have not been given.*
   6. *Do you know the woman ø I spoke to?*

CHAPITRE 18

P. 179 Exercice niveau 1
   2. 1. I'd like you to tell me what you saw or heard.
   2. Maybe you know what happened to your neighbour.
   3. I'm surprised to hear that you don't remember anything special.
   4. I don't believe what you're telling me.
   5. I don't think that you're telling me all that you know.

P. 181 Exercice niveau 1
   2. 1. I don't know how old he is.
   2. I don't think he's very old.
   3. Tell me what you think.
   4. I advise you not to move.
   5. I'm surprised that you came.
   4. Exercice niveau 2
   Nobody wants **their children** to live in a disintegrating planet. Yet it seems **that all forms of life are under threat**. Last week some of the most powerful companies held a meeting to decide **what they could do to save the planet**. Apparently the situation is different from **what it used to be**. The government now advises **companies to invest** in the production of lead-free petrol and uncontaminated food. The only problem is **that any form of environmental investment** costs money and British companies find it hard **to find the funds** to invest in environmental protection.

P. 183 Exercice niveau 1
   2. 1. - Why did he leave this morning?
      - Because he's found a better solution.
   2. - What did he phone you for?
      - To tell me to leave the door open.
   3. The maths test was so hard that I couldn't finish it.
   4. They cried out for everybody to hear them.
   Exercice niveau 2
   4. A footballing treasure has been lost!
   Neil Tinker announced his retirement from football yesterday **because of the injuries** he has had recently. He made his announcement on television **for everybody to know** the reason **why** he was doing it. "My retirement is really **due to** the fact that I've suffered badly through injury over the past two years. I'm certainly not **what** I was. I've often been blamed **for** not performing as I used to. And that's very frustrating."

P. 185 Exercice niveau 1
   2. 1. I don't know **whether** he's right or not.
   2. I wouldn't tell you **if** I wasn't sure!
   3. **If** you were not so silly, you would understand me.
   4. Don't speak **unless** you're sure of your answer.
   Exercice niveau 2
   4. 1. I'll leave early so that I won't be caught in the traffic.
   2. I don't know whether I should go or not.
   4. I'll go on speaking provided you don't interrupt me.
   5. Since you're refusing to speak to her, I don't see why she should stay.

Exercices niveau 2
  3. 1. b) Whatever
     2. c) whether
     3. b) what
     4. a) However
     5. c) how
  4. 1. (Al)though he was very tired, he went on working until dawn.
     2. He had never liked her whereas his brother had always found her very attractive.
     3. I have never read that book whereas my sister read it twice.
     4. (Al)though we tried our best to please our mother, she was never satisfied.
     5. I've never been to Italy, (al)though my daughter has been living there for three years now.

CHAPITRE 19

P. 189 Exercice niveau 1
  2. 1. I wonder whether she remembers me.
     2. Do you know whether she is leaving with Brandon?
     3. Tell me what happened.
     4. I want to know what you do on Saturdays.
     5. Can you tell me why she cried?
     Exercice niveau 2
  4. 1. She told me that she would ring him as soon as she got there.
     2. She explained to me that he couldn't see where she was going at the time.
     3. She asked me whether I would answer them.

P. 191 Exercice niveau 1
  2. 1. She asked me whether I liked her.
     2. They said that they would stay with him until the doctor arrived but he told them not to bother.
     3. I asked him whether he could lend me £50.
     Exercices niveau 2
  4. 1. She asked him whose boat it was.
     2. He answered that it was his father's.
     3. She asked him whether she knew his father.
     4. He said he did not think she did.
     5. She finally said that she'd rather stay where she was.
     6. He told her not to worry and said that they wouldn't be long.
  5. 1. He called him (her) a liar.
     2. He told him (her) to go away.
     3. He denied speaking to her.
     4. He suggested asking him.
     5. He advised him (her) to give up.

CHAPITRE 20

P. 195 Exercice niveau I

2. 1. My bags have been stolen.
   2. These tools are not used very often.
   3. We are being filmed.
   4. The president was murdered.

Exercices niveau 2

4. 1. He was being stared at.
   2. He is bound to be arrested.
   3. The problem will have to be dealt with.
   4. A bridge was being built.
   5. The doctor will have to be called for.
   6. He can't be relied on.
   7. She was being laughed at and made fun of.
   8. The council flats were being pulled down.

5. 1. The house had been broken into.
   2. Windows had been smashed and the furniture had been knocked down.
   3. Papers and books had been scattered all over the floor.
   4. Fortunately, no one had been assaulted.
   5. The act could not be accounted for because nothing had been taken away.

P. 197 Exercice niveau I

2. Matthew Arnold, a football fan **died** after he **was hit** during a match. Yesterday Barry Fox **was arrested** and **charged** with murder. He told the police: "I **hit** Matthew but I **didn't want** to kill him. Matthew **fell** to the ground but I **did not think** he **was injured**."

Exercices niveau 2

5. A 30-second earthquake **rocked** buildings and **shattered** windows in Los Angeles last night. Highway 118 **was heavily damaged**. A small shopping mall **was destroyed**. A fire **is believed** to **have been caused** by a fractured gas main. Hundreds of shops and cinemas **were evacuated**. 40 people **are reported** to **have been killed**.

6. **The measles vaccination is to be offered** to millions of children to combat an expected epidemic next year. Experts predict that **up to 200,000 children could be stricken by the disease**. The epidemic could reach levels not seen for more than a decade. **£20 million will be spent** on all children between 5 and 16. Epidemics affecting hundreds of thousands of victims were once common but **the toll was reduced by the introduction of the vaccine in 1968**. Chief Medical Officer Dr K C. said: "There is very strong evidence that **unless a strong immunisation campaign is carried out**, we will experience the largest measles epidemic since the early 1980s.

CHAPITRE 21

P. 199 Exercice niveau I

2. 1. *Who are you waiting **for**? Are you afraid **of** something?*
    Qui attends-tu ? Est-ce que tu as peur de quelque chose ?
    2. *Don't you agree **with** me? Do you disapprove **of** what I did?*
    Tu n'es pas d'accord avec moi ? Tu désapprouves ce que j'ai fait ?
    3. *Two men were accused **of** breaking **into** a house near the village of Dunbar. They were charged **with** robbery.*
    Deux hommes ont été accusés d'avoir cambriolé une maison tout près du village de Dunbar. Ils ont été inculpés de vol.
    4. *His parents never looked **after** him properly. I can't cope **with** him anymore! He's far too difficult!*
    Ses parents ne se sont jamais occupé de lui correctement. Je ne m'en sors plus ! Il est beaucoup trop difficile !
    5. *Have you heard **from** them lately? Did they phone or write? I look forward **to** seeing her again.*
    As-tu eu de leurs nouvelles récemment ? Ont-ils écrit ou téléphoné ? Il me tarde de la revoir.
    6. *You can't prevent her **from** seeing them! She's so fond of them.*
    Tu ne peux pas l'empêcher de les voir ! Elle a tellement d'affection pour eux.

    Exercice niveau 2

4. 1. *She was **under** the impression that we disliked her.*
    2. *You don't have to put **up** with him if he is so nasty.*
    3. *They have decided to put **off** the date of their wedding.*
    4. *I can't trust them. They have let me **down** so often.*

P. 201 Exercice niveau I

2. 1. *We're soon leaving **for** Italy.*
    2. *My children are looking **forward** to that.*
    3. *I hear you're going **to** Britain.*
    4. *Yes, I've been wanting to go there **for** a long time.*
    5. *You're the very person I was looking **for**.*
    6. *Who do you think you're talking **to**?*

    Exercice niveau 2

3. 1. *Please make **up** your mind quickly!*
    2. *He forgot to answer **ø** the last question.*
    3. *I don't think the old man will live **through** the night.*
    4. *Our neighbours' house was broken **into** during the night. The police are there now.*
    5. *Can I have a look **at** your painting?*
    6. *He did it **out of** anger.*
    7. *She was so sad that I didn't even try to cheer her **up**.*

P. 203 Exercice niveau I
1. 1. What's the use of asking **for** what you can't get?
   2. You say he's a famous writer, but I have never heard **of** him.
   3. That damn dog never obeys **ø** me!
   4. Please, do not enter **ø** my office without knocking.
   5. Our secret agent was accused **of** helping the enemy.
   6. He was very much interested **in** sports before he was sent there.

Exercice niveau 2
2. 1. No one thought of sending **for** the doctor.
   2. We all insisted **on** their staying.
   3. There's no point **in** arguing **about** my return to the States.
   4. The teacher was pleased **with** the pupils' results.
   5. The government should have another attitude **towards** education.
   6. A babysitter is responsible **for** the children he or she looks **after**.
   7. Please excuse me **for** not writing sooner.
   8. Have you congratulated him **on** his success?
   9. He at last succeeded **in** escaping from the camp.

P. 205 Exercice niveau I
1. 1. You should keep her **from** doing that; it's too dangerous.
   2. What do the initials UNESCO stand **for**?
   3. Would you please fill **in** this form.
   4. He came in from the rain and took **off** his wet clothes.
   5. That war has been going **on** for years.
   6. You did not answer **ø** his question!
   7. She is very good **at** languages.
   8. I don't approve **of** this marriage.

Exercices niveau 2
2. 1. He insisted **on** inviting me and I couldn't resist **ø** him.
   2. He gave **up** smoking last year.
   3. That doesn't account **for** the accident.
   4. They don't get on well **with** each other.
   5. He looks so much like his brother that he is often mistaken **for** him.
   6. We may play, but it will depend **on** the weather.
   7. Few people attended **ø** the meeting.
   8. He could not account **for** his foolish behaviour.
   9. What on earth is he crying **for (about)**?
3. 1. Stop **looking for** your glasses!
   2. I can't **go on** like this!
   3. He's **given up** drinking.
   4. He was **brought up** by his aunt.
   5. We can't **put up with** this!
   6. She **looks like** me.
4. 1. What does this sign **stand for**?
   2. Don't **go back** home!
   3. Don't **go into** the room!
   4. This has **brought about** much trouble.
   5. They have **cut down** the budget.
   6. They **turned down** my proposal.